*The
Connell Guide
to
The EU Referendum*

———

Stay or Go?

———

by Jane Lewis

Contents

NOTES

Britain's place in the world: the main arguments for and against Brexit

Mr Wilson takes a trip

In January 1967, the British Prime Minister, Harold Wilson, flew to Paris to re-open exploratory talks about joining the Common Market with the French President, General de Gaulle, who was then calling the shots in the fledgling six nation-strong alliance.

Outwardly, Britain was riding high. "In this century, every decade has its city... and for the Sixties that city is London," Time Magazine had proclaimed the previous year, heralding the arrival of "Swinging London" – the youthful, irrepressible home of everything "groovy". The social revolution mystified and angered older generations, clinging desperately to tradition. But the country had undeniably recovered its mojo for the first time since the war. The year that brought the world's "first psychedelic boutique" (Granny Takes a Trip, which opened on the Kings Road in February 1966), also saw England carry off that ultimate symbol of national feel-good, the Fifa World Cup.

Nonetheless, Wilson knew he was on the back foot with de Gaulle, then leading France through *les trente glorieuses* – the 30 years of post-war revival.

A developing crisis in Rhodesia (now Zimbabwe) served to underline Britain's post-imperial weakness. And beneath the beat of the boom, the UK economy was tanking: an ongoing sterling crisis would force Wilson into a full devaluation of the pound later that year. The PM's "discovery" of Europe, as the Daily Mirror's Hugh Cudlip put it at the time, was "a gigantic attempt to distract attention... from the economic mess at home".

To make matters worse, the notoriously prickly de Gaulle was hardly the most accommodating of negotiating partners. Distrustful of Britain's motives, he had vetoed the UK's first attempt to join the European Economic Community (EEC) in 1963, against the wishes of the group's five other members: Belgium, the Netherlands, Luxembourg, Italy and Germany.

To help charm the General, Wilson brought along his Foreign Secretary, the enthusiastically pro-European George Brown – which turned out to be a mistake. The official photographs of the meeting only seemed to emphasise Britain's diminished status, noted Wilson's biographer, Ben Pimlott. "De Gaulle towered sombrely over the two modestly proportioned British leaders as if symbolising the difference in world stature."

Pimlott recounts that the *pièce de résistance* of this spectacularly unsuccessful encounter was Brown's sozzled behaviour at an Embassy reception. In a "wearily familiar scene", he launched into a "foul-mouthed tirade" about the "alleged inefficiency of the staff". Wilson did his best to smooth things over, but couldn't keep his "tired and emotional" Foreign Secretary under control. "Back on the plane, Brown toured the secretarial quarters, chatting up the girls unrepentantly": revealing, as one aide observed, "that in this sense he had more of the human touch than Harold".

An unimpressed de Gaulle vetoed Britain's entry for a second time, maintaining, in a withering critique, that we had a "deep-seated hostility towards European construction". It took his fall from power in 1969, and his death a year later, to clear the way for Britain's entry in 1973.

No longer supplicants

Fifty years on, as we contemplate a new chapter in our European story, we might reflect that some things are reassuringly the same: not least Britain's relationship with our oldest and most beloved "frenemy". In April, an Odoxa poll for Le Parisien newspaper found that more French than British backed the idea of Brexit. Just 54% of French people were keen on *la perfide Albion* staying in the club (compared with 76% of Spaniards, 67% of Italians and 65% of Germans).

But, otherwise, a lot has changed. What was once a core industrial alliance has morphed into a super-bloc of 28 nations and 500 million souls, apparently inexorably bound towards ever-tighter political and economic union. Moreover, the geopolitical preoccupations of 1967 have been replaced by a new and equally daunting set of challenges: from a muscle-flexing Russia in the East, to the threat to European security and borders posed by Islamic terrorism, mass migration and the ongoing conflict in North Africa and the Middle East. The health of the global economy, meanwhile, is fragile. And there remains a live risk of financial implosion in the eurozone.

A big positive, from Britain's point of view, is that our own position vis-a-vis the EU has been transformed. As Matthew Parris noted in The Times in February, we approach not as "supplicants" this time, but from a comparative position of strength. Far from being the "Sick Man of Europe", "we are Europe's second-largest economy [after Germany] and the fifth biggest in the world". We're also the continent's biggest defence provider, and its most powerful member of Nato.

Indeed, for many continental allies, an EU without Britain is unthinkable. We offer a valuable counterweight to the "statist" tendencies of France and Germany, bringing much-needed Anglo-Saxon market grit; and we enhance the union's global clout. As one of Europe's "Big Three" states, the UK "routinely punches above its weight", writes Arthur Neslen in The Guardian. "Its size, imperial history, ceremony, financial clout and involvement in Europe over centuries bestow gravitas in Brussels."

The big fear in EU circles is that if Brexit encourages break-away rebels elsewhere, it could trigger further fissures at a dangerously unstable time, both within Europe – where rising levels of popular discontent have fuelled a worrying rise in political demagoguery – and without. "I worry most about the destructive forces that this could unleash," says the former Irish premier, John Bruton. "It is the potential of undoing 70 years of statesmanship."

"With or without us, the future of the European Union looks fragile," writes Parris. "Without us I'd predict disintegration" – a fracture that would "reverberate through this century" and "rock the West to its foundations".

> Carrying the weight we do, what would our storming out of the West's most important concert of nations do? A great wound would be inflicted to the clout that the continent of Europe carries, to the self-belief of European civilisation and to the image of Europe in the world... Would jihadists take fright – or heart – that European nations were dividing? Ask yourself how Putin and the Kremlin would view the news. Imagine the glee.

Quitting now, concludes Parris, would be "an abdication of responsibility... Brexit would mean that we don't give a damn."

Cry Freedom!

That argument, of course, is predicated on the assumption that the EU is a force for freedom, enlightenment and the advancement of democratic values – a laughable view in the eyes of the Leave camp. The European project might have started with high-minded intentions, says the Tory MP and justice minister, Dominic Raab, but Brussels has become "an increasingly authoritarian wolf in progressive sheep's clothing". Despite the various opt-outs that Britain has secured, the direction of travel is clear. We should get out while we can.

Far better, argue Remainers, to stay in Europe and push for reform from within. But what, really, are the chances of that? "Decisive and deliberate action would be necessary to put the EU on a different track," says Clive Crook on Bloomberg. "There's no sign of it." On the contrary, "momentum towards closer union is built into the system". Indeed for most of the union's members, closer political integration is actually necessary.

> Members of the euro area urgently need to develop a form of limited fiscal union, otherwise [the flaws] in the single currency will continue to hold them back. But the main force pushing further integration is institutional self-interest. The union has created powerful bodies – its parliament, executive and supreme court – with a huge vested interest in expanding their anti-

democratic competences under the union's malformed constitution. In the existing treaties, they already have everything they need to do that.

"The EU resists real reform partly because that would require treaty changes, which in some countries would then require popular ratification," adds Crook. Given growing anti-EU sentiment across the continent, any such endorsement may not be forthcoming, making it rash to consult them in the first place.

"This is how democracy works in Europe. The EU has over-reached, yet it's incapable of fixing the error."

A question of identity

The trouble with the EU, writes Merryn Somerset Webb in the Financial Times, is that "most of us feel no real connection or belief in it. We care about it only in terms of what we can get out of it. That makes it a deeply uncertain construct to be attached to."

Geographically, historically and, to large extent, culturally, Britain is a European country. But it's far from our only identity in the world. Indeed, the central question that confronted Wilson in 1967 – and has bedevilled almost every British PM since – is broadly the same. With whom do our loyalties, as an island nation that has always projected outwards into the world, really lie?

Winston Churchill and General Charles de Gaulle in Paris on 11 November 1944

Before his pragmatic pro-Europe conversion, Harold Wilson thought that Britain's future lay with the Commonwealth, observes Ben Pimlott.

It was possible to see the Commonwealth, not as a sentimental association, or even just a trading area, but as a multi-racial community and potential force in the world... in which there was a post-colonial role for Britain, guiding the development of poorer nations. Entry into Europe, Wilson believed, would mean sacrificing that opportunity.

No one talks about "post-colonial" development any more. Nonetheless, the view that Britain should shrug off EU constraints and strut its stuff globally is central to the Eurosceptic case. Why not play to past strengths? Because of (or perhaps despite) our imperial past, we enjoy unique historical, cultural ties with many emerging (and emerged) economies in Asia, Africa and elsewhere. Given that millions of modern Britons trace their heritage to those countries, there are blood ties too. With the balance of economic power shifting rapidly towards these new players, we should make the most of these connections.

Much the same is said of Britain's other private club: the so-called "Anglosphere". The idea, popularised by the historian Robert Conquest, is that the answer to Britain's growing "democratic deficit" in Europe is a "more fruitful unity" with other English-speaking nations – the USA, Australia, Canada and New Zealand, whose free market values and political institutions are much more in tune with our own.

These claims have often been met with derision. "For international relations realists, the idea of an Anglosphere barely merits a straight face, let alone serious consideration," argues Nick Pearce, Professor of Public Policy at the University of Bath.

But the Anglosphere's potency is ideological, not geopolitical. It functions as an imaginary horizon for a eurosceptic worldview of Britain after

Brexit, uniting the UK with a global trading future as well as a sceptered isle past. It registers nostalgia, but also energy. Britain would be liberated to march on the world stage again, freed from sclerotic, conformist Europe and reanimated by the animal spirits that once gave it an empire. Thus it defends the eurosceptic flank where it is most vulnerable – rebutting the charge that it wants to take Britain back to the 1950s by delving even deeper into our island story and casting it forward into the 21st century.

Yet there is no denying that much of the basic anatomy of Britain remains incompatible with the European project. As the world's most mature democracy, our evolutionary, unwritten constitution – dating back to Magna Carta and sprawling out, as romantics like to say, like the roots of a gnarly British oak – is completely at odds with the more codified approach prevalent in much of continental Europe. The same is true of our system of Common Law. "The British have the distinction above all others of being able to put new wine into old bottles without breaking them," the post-war PM, Clement Atlee, once said.

Britain can trace its rise as a global power from the 16th century onwards to a talent for nimbleness and opportunism. With established world orders crumbling and new powers rising, what better time to shrug off the dead weight of Europe? As Martin Vander Weyer concluded in The Spectator in

March: "There is a world of opportunity out there for a resurgent UK in command of our own destiny."

Keep a-hold of Nurse?

As is often observed, the Brexiteers have all the best tunes. How much more stirring is their swashbuckling vision of Britannia resurgent abroad – and returned to true democratic accountability at home – than the grim future painted if Britain remains in the clutches of the EU?

"British Eurosceptics have badmouthed the EU for the past 20 years, and have largely won the argument. Public opinion in the UK is divided into two groups: those who hate the EU and want to get out and those who want, reluctantly to stay, citing some putative economic advantage," writes the FT commentator, Wolfgang Munchau. The pro-EU arguments are uninspiring – "bean-counting exercises in computing hypothetical costs and benefits" – leaving the way clear for Leave campaigners "to argue on political and emotional grounds".

The most extreme version of the Remainers' "utilitarian argument" is "Project Fear": the idea that the only way to garner support from voters is to scare them into submission. Brexiteers are fond of taunting their opponents with the famous Hilaire Belloc line: "Always keep a-hold of Nurse for fear of finding something worse." But actually, Pro-Europeans are quite right to stress that Brexit would be a leap in the dark. No one knows what would actually happen.

The Out camp might insist that any short-term ructions are a price worth paying to regain control. But what about the picture long-term? Would the UK really have any influence in a world increasingly dominated by regional trading blocs and multinational companies? The fact that almost all our major trading partners and allies have expressed support for Britain's continued membership of the EU should surely tell us something.

The Brexiteers believe in "a myth of British exceptionalism", writes David Marquand on OpenDemocracy.net. "It's time they stopped telling themselves fairy tales." They see the UK "as a uniquely freedom-loving country besting continental tyrants". But the truth is that "Britain outside the EU would be a meaner, nastier and more inward-looking place. Indeed, the overwhelming probability is that 'Britain' would no longer exist." Brexit would likely trigger another Scottish bolt for independence, and Wales could well follow suit. We'd be left with a decapitated rump: "A market society governed by a market state, presiding over a glorified tax haven and financial services hub."

Besides, we tend to overlook that the European project has actually been rather good for Britain: we've enjoyed the fruits of 70 years of peace on the continent and our economy has prospered. The Out camp might counter that that is merely coincidental – if things are good, think how much better they would be freed of the constraints of Brussels. Yet one of the big problems we face when weighing the pros and cons of EU membership is that many of the benefits it confers have become invisible – subsumed into everyday life. We take them for granted, but would miss them dearly if they vanished or had to be renegotiated.

Pro-Europeans argue that Britain already enjoys the best of both worlds from our existing "semi-detached" relationship. We are in the EU, with the influence to shape it from within, but we maintain our own currency and border controls – an enviable strategic position. We have carved out a unique role as a user-friendly bridgehead to the European market for the rest of the world, and have prospered mightily from it. Were you playing a geopolitical version of the board-game Risk, you might conclude that Britain has a perfect opening position. Why throw away that advantage?

Make your mind up time

The problem with reaching any conclusion about the wisdom, or otherwise, of staying in the EU is the relentless barrage of facts and figures thrown at us daily. The two sides have made a cottage industry of disputing statistics that contradict their arguments, and accuse each other of scare tactics. But, as Daniel Finkelstein says in the Times, "even where the facts are agreed it is possible to see them in different ways, all of them persuasive". The sad truth is that there is "no unbiased authority" to adjudicate, or tell us what might actually happen if Britain votes to leave.

You'll just have to do your best based on a bit of common sense, your natural balance between adventurousness and caution, your decision about how much you respect the judgement of people on either side and your view about Britain's place in the world.

A FEW FACTS AND FIGURES

"I love Europe! France is wonderful. It should be. We've subsidised it for 40 years"

Nigel Farage

How much Britain gets and receives from the EU
Britain sends £350m a week or £18bn a year to Brussels.

Subtract from that:

The UK's rebate on contributions:	£5bn
EU farming subsidies and regional development funds:	£4.5bn
EU grants to the private sector	£1.4bn

These reductions reduce Britain's weekly contribution to £136m – equating to an annual spend just over £7bn a year.

(Source: Financial Times)

Total UK Government Expenditure 2016-17 is forecast at £772bn

(Source: Office for Budget Responsibility)

Costliest EU legislation (per annum)

*UK Renewable Energy Strategy:	£4.7bn
*Capital Requirements Directive (prudential rules for banks etc)	£4.6bn
*The Working Time Directive	£4.2bn
*The EU Climate and Energy Package	£3.4bn
*Temporary Agency Workers Directive	£2.1bn

(Source: Open Europe 2015)

Cost to UK of EU regulation

The eurosceptic economist, Tim Congdon, put the total cost of the UK's EU membership in 2015 at around 12% of GDP, or slightly more than £190bn – much of that caused by the damage of "excessive and misguided regulation".

(Source: Ukip research 2015)

Many dispute the figure. As economist David Smith of The Sunday Times points out: "Britain already has one of the most deregulated product and labour markets in the world, according to the OECD. Besides, much of the red tape is home-grown: "HMRC does not get its instructions from Brussels." Indeed, the UK tax code "is ten times the length of that in Germany", says Simon French of Panmure Gordon.

Benefits of EU membership

According to a study by the pro-EU business group, the CBI, a "conservative" estimate of the benefits of EU membership amounted to 4.5% of GDP, or around £78bn a year, making each UK household £3,000 better off.

(Source: Confederation of British Industry 2013)

Impact of Brexit on jobs: 3 million?

The figure often bandied around is that 3 million UK jobs, "linked" to exports to the EU, could be lost. But it's based on "heroic assumptions", says Chris Giles in the *FT*. No "sensible forecasts" show all jobs linked to EU exports are in danger. "That would assume Britain stops trading altogether with the EU after Brexit."

The sectors most under threat are probably the car industry and financial services, notes Katie Allen in The Guardian.

The Society of Motor Manufacturers and Traders has argued that Europe is fundamental to sectors employing more than 700,000. But, as a KPMG report cautions: "there are no guarantees they would leave". Indeed, the Japanese car-maker, Toyota, has stated it is committed to keeping UK operations intact if Britain votes to leave.

In financial services, several large international banks have hinted they would quit Britain if it pulled out, including America's largest bank, JP Morgan, which employs 16,000. Whether they would act in the event is another matter. Much would depend on the outcome of the UK's negotiations with the EU.

The Institute of Economic Affairs, a free market think-tank, believes reports of big job losses are over-egged.

> Jobs are associated with trade, not membership of a political union, and there is little evidence that trade would substantially fall between British businesses and European consumers.

It also notes the UK labour market is dynamic and so would adjust.

> Prior to the financial crisis, the UK saw on average 4m jobs created and 3.7m jobs lost each year – showing how common substantial churn of jobs is

at any given time. The annual creation and destruction of jobs is almost exactly the same scale as the estimated 3-4m jobs that are associated with exports to the EU.

(Source: The EU Jobs Myth, IEA (2015))

Impact on foreign direct investment

The UK is the number one destination in Europe for foreign direct investment (FDI). Accountancy firm EY provides the most comprehensive annual survey of FDI. Its 2015 report showed a record 887 inward investment projects in Britain in 2014, up 11% on the previous year, and an increased European market share of 20.4%. According to EY, 72% of investors cited access to the single market as important in their decision.

(Source: EY 2015 UK attractiveness survey.)

HOW THE EU WORKS

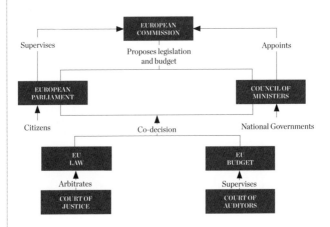

The three main institutions of the European Union – the European Commission, the Council of Ministers and the European Parliament – form the framework for co-operation between its 28 member states.

Here's what they do, and how they interact.

The European Council

Current President: Donald Tusk, former PM of Poland

Composed of the heads of government of member countries, the Council's main role is to define the EU's general political direction and priorities: for instance, it's responsible for setting common foreign and security policies. Essentially a top echelon talking shop – leaders generally meet for quarterly summits – it's a useful forum for tackling complex or sensitive issues that cannot be resolved further down the chain. Crucially, the council does not pass laws, but it is responsible for appointing the members of the European Commission which does. It also appoints the heads of other important EU institutions like the European Central Bank.

The European Commission

Current President: Jean-Claude Juncker

The EU's main legislative body is made up of a team or "college" of commissioners: one from each EU country, usually appointed by the head of government. The commission submits its proposals for approval by the Council of Ministers and the European Parliament – the only body with the power to sack Commissioners. As well as proposing and enforcing legislation, it sets the EU's spending priorities, draws up budgets and negotiates international agreements. Britain's commissioner is Lord (Jonathan) Hill – a former PR man, who was John Major's political secretary during the Maastricht Treaty negotiations (see Timeline) and is considered "business-friendly". Juncker has given Hill responsibility for financial services.

The European Parliament

Current President: Martin Schulz

The parliament, which unlike the other two Brussels-based institutions is based in Strasbourg, consists of 751 MEPs, directly elected by EU voters every five years. Its main role is the democratic scrutiny of all EU institutions – in particular, the Commission. It elects the latter's president, approves the Commission as a body, and scrutinises legislation which, if happy, it passes. It also decides on international agreements and EU enlargement. But critics say it lacks real teeth.

European Agencies

Beneath the umbrella of the main EU institutions, there is a raft of smaller EU agencies, dotted across the Continent, dedicated to running every aspect of European life: from the European Police Office (Europol), to the Dublin-based European Foundation for the Improvement of Living and Working Conditions and the European Medicines Agency in Parma. ∎

Sources: Europa, the BBC

The tribes in Parliament

> "I'm veering all over the place like a shopping trolley."
>
> *Boris Johnson, February 2016*

Europe has always been a toxic issue in British politics – not just because it causes division between parties but because of the lethal fissures it causes within them, says the constitutional historian, Professor Vernon Bogdanor.

> Some might argue that the fundamental conflict in post-war politics is not so much between left and right as between those who believe that Britain's future lies with Europe and those who believe it does not.

In the early years of Britain's membership, the Tories were remarkably united about the benefits of the European Economic Community (or the Common Market as it was known) – probably because the emphasis in the June 1975 referendum was so firmly placed on trade. Margaret Thatcher, who had toppled Ted Heath to take the party's leadership a few months earlier, was, as Dominic Lawson recalls in The Sunday Times, the campaign's chief cheerleader, "happily wearing a pullover festooned with the flags of member states".

Back then, it was the Labour party that was torn apart by the EEC, which was viewed by many on the left as a "capitalist club", notes the Times columnist Daniel Finkelstein. Now the deep split is in the Conservative party. By mid-March, 140 Tory MPs (out of 330) had declared for Leave: "more than even the most optimistic" in the Brexit camp had expected, noted The Economist. The PM's Remain campaign, however, has had precious little help from either supposedly pro-EU Labour or the Scottish Nationalists, partly because neither can stomach sharing a platform with the hated Tories.

Of course, there are other reasons. The SNP "knows that a vote for Brexit could be an excuse for another independence referendum". And although Labour's parliamentary party and its grass-roots are overwhelmingly pro-EU, the leader, Jeremy Corbyn, is a longstanding eurosceptic whose strategy, on the whole, has been to keep shtum.

Westminster politicians, as Dominic Lawson ruefully notes, have always used rows about the EU to further their own ends at the ballot box. Not much has changed. But this campaign has also been remarkable for the disagreements on strategy exposed within the two camps. Particularly on the subject of fear. Were ominous predictions of apocalypse a turn-off to voters, or a key weapon in the debate? Neither political scientists nor politicians could agree. As the pro-EU Conservative MP, Nicholas Soames told Prospect:

I don't know which ass – and ass is the most moderate word that I can think of – thought of the name 'Project Fear' but there is no such thing... [The term] was probably invented by some little twerp in a think tank.

...and in the country

Despite a clamour for "facts" at the start of the campaign, a Populus poll found that the traditional British *ennui* when it comes to discussing the EU's workings hadn't shifted much. Only 28% thought they could explain to a friend what sovereignty means; 20% could explain the single market; 14% the Schengen agreement; and 17% the concept of an ever-closer union.

But this apathy was more than matched by strength of feeling. Where you stood on Europe, it was often observed, was a tribal thing – and that sometimes meant civil war within established groups.

"For the first time in my life my like-minded friends are riven with argument over a voting issue," wrote one Spectator reader. "It is impossible to ignore the elephant in the room. How can one best navigate this unwelcome tempest and remain friends both before and, more importantly, after the referendum?"

The best advice, replied the magazine's etiquette aunt, Mary Killen, was to treat guests who wished to discuss Brexit like smokers: they were welcome to indulge, but only outside where "the discomfort of the chilly nether regions" allowed arguments to be swiftly wound up.

Tribe anatomy

Neil Collins, also writing in The Spectator, skewered two disagreeable-sounding types of "Stayers" – wrongheaded do-gooders and smug plutocrats.

> They are, by and large, the sort of agreeable, liberal people who... thought the pain of the ERM worthwhile and advocated the single currency for Britain. They are also, if you like, the great and the good: the Davos elite of bankers, international corporate chiefs and europhiles for whom the status quo is just fine, thanks.

The "Leavers", by contrast, "seem a more disparate bunch", noted Collins,

> from pull-up-the-drawbridge Little Englanders to those who, more in sorrow than anger, see the EU as irretrievably broken and so far from its free-trade-zone origins as to be unrecognisable...

A big theme of the Out camp was that it stood for the put-upon, striving classes whose voices went unheard. It was all about "the little people" versus "vested interests". Thus the former boss of the British Chambers of Commerce, John Longworth – ousted in March for his eurosceptic views – invoked the spirit of the 14th century Peasants Revolt, casting himself as a latter-day Wat Tyler against an Establishment that is "ruthless in defence of its own interests".

> There are Eurocrats and those in the "EU-invested" business and political elite... who consider "the little people" to be irrelevant in this referendum campaign, That the "little people" can be manipulated... What they forget is that it is the "little people", and I consider myself among them, who do most of the work, pay their taxes, underpin the consumption economy and suffer unemployment in downturns. It is the individual entrepreneurs who risk their own money and sweat blood to create most of the jobs... This merry band will vote to leave the EU in June and be free of its shackles.

The business vote is rather more nuanced than Longworth allows. And his resort to *ye olde pageant of historie* taps into a central weakness of the Out campaign – the perception that Brexiteers are a bunch of saloon bar bores and/or reactionary nutcases, tinged with socially regressive Ukip-ish views. And that, like Ukip, they're permanently at war with one other. As The Economist put it:

> Leavers are vulnerable not just to uncertainty over what alternative they would secure, but to their own disagreements. The way the two groups [Grassroots Out and Vote Leave] now pour more vitriol on each other than on their

Margaret Thatcher speaking at a meeting of the party's campaign to keep Britain in the Common Market, watched by her predecessor Edward Heath, on 17th May 1975

opponents is comically reminiscent of the rival popular fronts to liberate Judaea in the film *The Life of Brian.*

But the polls show that euroscepticism in Britain enjoys far broader support than this rather narrow depiction allows. A deciding factor for many is the EU's impact on their own livelihoods. To take two extreme examples, the fishing industry, which views itself a victim of the worst kind of Brussels diktat ("They've taken our fish!") is, almost to a boat, in the Out camp, while much of Britain's farming industry – reliant on generous EU subsidies and cheap migrant labour – quite naturally takes the opposite tack. "Anyone running a farm would have to be either mad, or incredibly driven by democratic principle, to vote Leave," says one Norfolk farmer. (See Common Agricultural Policy and Common Fisheries Policy in Glossary, p.95)

An Economist poll of polls in mid-April found that the Leave campaign was playing slightly better in the North (40% Brexit vs 34% Remain) than the South. It also uncovered a high level of support among manual workers and the unemployed, who arguably have most to lose from any frontline squeeze on jobs, housing and services. Immigration was the key issue on the streets of Romford, the Essex town identified by YouGov as the most "eurosceptic" in the country, reported Stephen Moss in The Guardian. The most pro-EU was Aberystwyth, which ticked two europhile heartland boxes: as a "cosmopolitan" university town surrounded by a rural community dependent on EU grants.

The youth vote

What really leaps out of all the data, though, is "the striking contrast in attitudes towards Europe between the generations", said Andrew Rawnsley in The Observer. While it's "neck-and-neck" among the middle-aged, there's "a landslide for staying in" among the under-35s: 53% would stay in, while just 29% were for Brexit, an opinion poll in April found. For those aged 55 and over, the figures "are almost exactly reversed".

You could see it as an inversion of the usual stereotypes about age. It is wild oldsters who want to take a leap into the unknown by self-ejecting from the world's largest trading area, and it is level-headed youngsters who prefer the security of the status quo.

The big nightmare for Remain, notes Rawnsley, is that oldsters are much more likely to vote: more than 80% of the over-55s declare they are "absolutely certain" to vote in the referendum, compared with barely more than half of the under 35s. And it may not bode well either that the vote coincides with Glastonbury. "Decisions are made by those who turn up," concludes Rawnsley. "For all the breath that the Prime Minister has expended telling people that this may be the most important vote they ever cast, the message is clearly not getting through."

The problem, as one newly-qualified voter, Wilf Bairamian, outlines, is a lack of engagement. "There's the perception that what the EU does is relatively dull: it's difficult to get excited about fisheries policies... And I don't think many of my friends are aware of what they stand to lose if we come out of the EU." An important consideration for a well-travelled generation, facing the prospect of unaffordable living costs in Britain, is that Brexit might mean losing an easy passport to building a life elsewhere in Europe. "That's the big problem with the Out argument. 'The EU will give us a great deal,' they say. But where's the evidence? No one in the Leave campaign seems to have a clear strategy of how things would work if we came out."

The third tribe

If the youth vote is crucial in a tight campaign, so too is a sizeable third tribe – the Undecideds. With the polls showing that between a fifth and quarter of women are still wavering (compared with around 12% of men), they are a crucial group to be wooed. Hence, perhaps, the sudden interest in tampons that both sides discovered in March, when the Government headed off a eurosceptic back-bench rebellion in the nick of time by persuading Brussels to relax its rules on VAT. "We heard people's anger over paying the tampon tax loud and clear," said the Chancellor, George Osborne. "It just shows how Britain can make a case for a reform that will benefit millions as a powerful, confident voice inside a reformed EU."

Arguments like this, however, can sometimes backfire. No one seemed very convinced, for example, by the Remain camp's "Talk to Gran" campaign – which urged the young to convert the old via a series of patronising post cards. ("Nan, let's sit down for a cuppa, a slice of Battenberg and a chat about why my future's in the EU."). "Heaven help the young – mostly university students apparently – at whom this call is aimed," says Janet

Daley in The Sunday Telegraph. "Talk to Gran in terms like that and you will probably get more than you bargained for."

> It is worth asking just how out of touch you have to be to presuppose that everybody over the age of 60 who plans to vote Leave is a dotty uninformed dimwit. Never mind the assumption that the older generation might be planning to vote for Leave without giving a second thought to the welfare of their children and grandchildren, which presumably makes them selfish as well as ignorant.

Where's the plan?

The Remain camp's chief weakness, when addressing the Undecided, is the lack of a simple, compelling, positive message, argues Gideon Rachman in the Financial Times.

> The Leave campaign has the advantage of simple slogans that are easy to understand: control our borders, make our own laws, get our money back from Brussels. The Remain campaign's responses to these demands, by contrast, are complicated. They point out that, if Britain wants to retain full access to the EU single market, it will almost certainly have to accept free movement of people as the price of entry, along with single-market regulations. They explain that, while Britain's

contribution to the EU budget sounds like a big number, it is actually a very small part of overall government spending. These are intellectually solid arguments. But they are also unhelpfully convoluted. And in politics, as the saying goes: "If you are explaining, you are losing."

Yet there is also a glaring hole in the Leave camp. A large group of Undecideds declare themselves "emotionally" committed to leaving the EU, but fear taking the plunge because as the actor, Tom Conti, complained, "no-one has a plan" for how Britain would operate in the world post-Brexit.

"Oh God," sighed Boris Johnson audibly, when tackled on the point by an opponent on a radio talk show. "Look, stop running this country down. The sheer negativity rises off the Remain campaign like a vapour."

Maybe so. But with the polls running neck-and-neck as the official campaign got under way, it was clear that Leave's ability to rise to this challenge would have a decisive effect on the final outcome. Britain's EU membership, as The Economist concluded, was "hanging by a thread".

D.I.V.O.R.C.E

Picture the scene, says Gideon Rachman in the Financial Times. "It is the morning of June 24th 2016 and Britain has just voted narrowly to leave the EU."

Jubilant pro-Brexit campaigners wave Union Jacks in Trafalgar Square.

A shattered-looking David Cameron appears outside 10 Downing Street to say that he respects the verdict of the British people and that he intends to carry on as prime minister. The atmosphere of crisis is compounded by a stock market plunge across Europe.

In the days that follow, the Conservative party is consumed with in-fighting and it becomes clear that the Prime Minister's authority is too badly damaged for him to continue. The Tory party elder statesman Ken Clarke's prophecy that "the PM won't last 30 seconds" is fulfilled. In the ensuing leadership election, Boris Johnson defeats George Osborne and is invited to form a government. What next?

Firing the Lisbon starting gun

No other EU member has ever quit the union so it's largely a matter of conjecture – there is no precedent. But there is a framework of sorts. To leave the EU, Britain will have to trigger an exit clause – Article 50 of the 1987 Lisbon Treaty. The joke among Brussels insiders is that the clause was "designed never to be used": it has gaps and is unclear in places. But once that button is hit, the clock starts ticking. Britain would have two years to negotiate the terms of its departure from the EU and agree new trading arrangements with scores of other countries whose markets we currently have access to via the union, including the US, China and India.

Gung-ho factions in the Brexit camp tend to gloss over the complexity of this operation. But the deadline looks tight, to say the least – particularly considering the snail's pace at which trade talks usually progress. Negotiations on the EU's new trade deal with Canada began in 2009, yet it still hasn't been ratified. And that was just one deal.

To fulfil the terms of Lisbon, Britain would have to complete the process in double-quick time. A tall order, says Stephen Weatherill, professor of European law at Oxford University.

"People talk about the EU as if it were a monolith," he told the Financial Times in February.

"In fact, the UK will be negotiating with the commission, with 27 member states, with the European parliament, national parliaments, with their electorates. There are a lot of veto players here. They'll be herding cats to get these actors to agree."

Article 50, and all that

Under the circumstances, maybe it would be easier just to forget about Article 50 – or, at any rate, kick it down the road. That, after all, is how business in Europe is done; there's a long and dishonourable history of it. Consider how many times Greece avoided Acropolis Now because a loophole was found to delay a debt deadline.

Some of the more serious thinkers in Vote Leave argue that a Lisbon fudge is certainly the best way to secure a smooth Brexit – including Britain's senior justice minister, the Lord Chancellor, Michael Gove. His plan is simple: don't hit the button! Or at least, not till you're ready to. Much better to have "preliminary, informal conversations" with the rest of the EU "to explore how best to proceed" first.

This marks a clear divide with David Cameron's view that Article 50 would have to be invoked immediately if Britain voted to leave. It's what he agreed with other EU heads of state and has been accepted by the European Council. Gove disagrees: "The process of change is in our hands," he says. "It would not be in any nation's interest artificially to accelerate the process, and no responsible government would hit the start button."

Dominic Cummings, a former advisor to Gove and Vote Leave strategist, puts it more brutally. Invoking Article 50, he says,

> would be like putting a gun in your mouth and pulling the trigger... No one in their right mind would begin a legally defined-two year maximum period to conduct negotiations before they actually knew, roughly speaking, what this process was going to yield.

Britain, in other words, would negotiate to negotiate: for however long it took to extract favourable terms. Even though Boris Johnson has rejected the idea, many in Vote Leave still think an Out vote could be used as a bargaining chip to negotiate a better settlement for Britain, which could then be decided upon by the country in a second referendum.

The more hardline Leave.eu faction of the Out camp hates this idea of a phony Brexit, viewing it as a sell-out and a betrayal of the cause. "Article 50 stipulates we must leave within two years. True Brexiteers might see this as a guarantee of freedom," writes Liam Deacon on the libertarian website, Breitbart. Ignoring the treaty's terms is merely an attempt by "soft Eurosceptics" to "get undecided voters on side".

> Instead of immediately embracing our newfound sovereignty and ability to build international relationships, this camp appears to want to put everything on ice and find a middle path.

Any post-Brexit British Government could expect trouble at home if it went ahead with this plan. The far more important question is whether our spurned former EU partners would play along. Leaving the EU might be Britain's choice, but that doesn't mean we can dictate the exit terms.

A friendly divorce?

It seems rather odd that "eurosceptics, of all people, should rest their case on the friendship and fair-mindedness of other EU governments", says Clive Crook on Bloomberg. We probably could "agree a friendly divorce" that would preserve most of the union's mutual single-market benefits but allow Britain to step aside from the political project, if other members wanted it. But what are the chances of that?

> Eroding national sovereignty is one of the EU's declared purposes – its manifest destiny, if you will. Europe's other governments won't help Britain prove the viability of... less political integration. The split wouldn't be friendly, and Europe is in a position to make Britain pay.

The question of what the UK is worth to Europe in terms of trade has been hotly debated. But whatever the exact balance of power, Brexiters argue that it wouldn't be in the EU's interest to make life difficult for the UK to access the single market.

"They're right about where Europe's *economic* interests would lie," says Crook.

> But that isn't the point. Some EU governments would be happy to harm themselves slightly to hurt Britain a lot – you know, *pour encourager les autres*... The UK has a lot to lose if the EU

decided to be unaccommodating, and I'm betting the EU would.

Striking a deal would be like "arranging a divorce on advantageous terms with an embittered spouse". And it would be a long, drawn out affair. Senior EU and British officials reckon total divorce could take a decade to achieve.

"Ask any divorced couple whether their relationship would have been different had they never married," says Anatole Kaletsky, writing in Prospect. "Actually, don't bother, the answer is obvious." That's why it's bonkers to assume that if we voted Out we could blithely "produce a relationship similar to, but better than, the EU's deals with Switzerland and Norway".

There is a world of difference between politely declining a marriage proposal, as Norway and Switzerland have done repeatedly since the 1970s, and acrimoniously breaking up a prosperous, if difficult, relationship that has lasted for 40 years.

Indeed, observers report that tempers are already running short. "What I pick up in Brussels and other EU capitals is a palpable sense of British betrayal and a growing determination that the farce of British exceptionalism has got to stop before the risk of disintegration spreads," says former Liberal MEP Andrew Duff, now a visiting fellow at the European

Policy Centre. Wolfgang Schäuble, Germany's famously intransigent finance minister, made much the same point in April. If Britain voted Out, he said, it could expect negotiations to be "tough".

A whiff of fatalism

Of course Schäuble would say that, wouldn't he? He's a paid-up new member of Project Fear. And you could just as easily argue the point the other way. Senior EU politicians may bluster, but it's just as likely that Brussels would be forced into a more accommodating relationship with Britain, post-Brexit – to prevent an economic shock hastening what some see as the inevitable collapse of an unsustainable construct.

"Populist movements whose leaders believe they will benefit from Brexit are on the rise across Europe," observed Natalie Nougayrade in The Guardian. "Fragmentation is spreading every-where." And there's "a whiff of fatalism in the air, or at least a careless passivity [that] makes the situation especially dangerous".

Of course, Cassandras have been wrong before about the European project, she adds. "But in this age of extremes... moderate voices are fast drowned out by radical voices." For months I thought that Britain leaving the EU was unlikely – so did most European leaders. But "I've started thinking the unthinkable about Brexit".

Trade winds

"Free trade agreements do not come free, do not cover all trade and take ages to agree."

Lord (Peter) Mandelson,
former EU trade commissioner

Trade is at the heart of the European Union. It was the impetus of its formation, and the key driver of the continent's post-war recovery and prosperity. So why not return to the purity of that original relationship? It's what the British public agreed to in the 1975 referendum and, as things stand, we

AMERICA, "THE OTHER WOMAN"

"For years – no, decades – the anti-EU camp has suggested that Britain's natural habitat is not among its continental neighbours but in 'the Anglosphere'," says Jonathan Freedland in The Guardian: "that solar system of English-speaking planets which revolves around the United States".

The Brexit camp has long been like the man who dreams of leaving his wife for another woman, one who really understands him.

"Obama," says Freedland, "is that other woman." And on his spring visit to London, the US President shattered the outers' fantasies. His message was unambiguous. "Don't rush into a hasty divorce because you think we're waiting for you with open arms. We're not." America has no intention of forming a new closer relationship with a Brexited Britain. On the contrary, the UK would be at "the back of the queue" if it sought to agree its own, new trade treaty.

don't exactly get the best of deals from Europe's single market anyway.

The EU might account for around 44% of UK exports, but Britain's real forte is services: everything from legal and professional expertise to our thriving creative industries and the City of London, the world's greatest financial centre. But services are the one part of the single market that remains resolutely incomplete. Typical, say Brexiters. It certainly gives the lie to George Osborne's claim that Britain has an excellent record of reforming the EU from within.

The intervention infuriated Vote Leavers, like Boris Johnson. America, they say, would never accept the limitations on sovereignty demanded of Britain by the EU. But the comparison is "silly", counters Freedland. "Britain is strong and rich, but it is also a relatively small country adjacent to a continent. The US virtually *is* a continent." Besides, America does "trim its sovereignty" when it suits its purposes. For instance, it agrees to be bound by the rulings of the World Trade Organisation and Nafta, even though that sometimes means countermanding Congress's decisions.

The chief consolations of this disastrous presidential visit for the Out camp are that a) Obama's remarks looked like they were "crafted" in Downing Street and that b) he's on his way out anyway. "This is really about a lame duck US president... doing an old British friend [David Cameron] a favour," said Justice Minister, Dominic Raab. Given looming US elections in November, whatever Obama says is "largely irrelevant", agreed the former Tory defence secretary, Liam Fox. "It will be the next President, and the next Congress, who will be in charge of any trade arrangements." ∎

Anarchy in the UK

It should also make us think about what kind of trading nation we are, and how that tallies with our continued membership of the EU. As Janan Ganesh observes in the Financial Times, we don't always recognise "the quiet success of Britain's anarchic economic model" with its strong "anti-interventionist" bent.

"France cherishes its managed market as an expression of the national *idée fixe*: that good things must be organised, not left to chance." Germany's exporting prowess "has given it something more innocuous than blood and soil from which to derive an identity". Alone among Europe's three largest nations, "Britain has prospered – while faintly cringing – at the financial skew of its economy".

It's rather a myth that the UK doesn't make things, adds Ganesh: we're brilliant at high-end technical stuff – industrial lenses, aerospace gizmos and the like. Yet ultimately, our strength in services may prove the best bet as the world's "new economies" mature.

> Germany's stunted service sector may turn out to be a historic miscalculation if the profile of Chinese demand morphs from manufactured goods to the insurance, banking and legal counsel demanded by an increasingly sophisticated looking economy.

Indeed, a 2012 Goldman Sachs research note forecast that on present trends Britain could be on course to overtake Germany as Europe's largest economy by mid-century.

Hoist the mainsail

The other quite remarkable thing about Britain, says Bagehot in The Economist, is how "strikingly comfortable" we are with the concept of free trade compared with other big western economies. Perhaps that isn't surprising given our history as a maritime power. Even so, the figures are arresting.

An international survey by YouGov last year put net agreement that "free trade is good for business" at +6% among Americans, +3% among Germans, and at -4% among the French. In Britain the figure was +40%.

What's more, the research suggests that young Britons are even keener on free markets than older generations. This positive attitude is reflected in the Referendum campaign where, remarkably, both sides "squabble over which outcome would do more to lower trade barriers". It's hard to imagine any other country behaving like that. On the contrary, voters elsewhere in the West seem to be demanding the reinforcement of borders, both physical and economic. From everything we've heard so far, it is certainly what a Trump presidency in America would entail.

Seductive Singapore

Left to its own devices, then, perhaps Britain could flourish as a kind of Singapore of Europe. When the think-tank, Open Europe, analysed the various potential Brexit outcomes in a 2015 study, *What If*, it concluded that a Singapore-type arrangement would be "best case scenario" for Britain in terms of future growth. If we struck a Free Trade Agreement with the EU, pursued "very ambitious deregulation" of the economy and opened up "almost fully to trade with the rest of the world", British GDP would be 1.6% higher than if we stayed in the EU.

This idea of a future beyond Europe isn't just wishful thinking. It's already happening, argues the eurosceptic Daily Telegraph and Moneyweek columnist, Matthew Lynn. The British economy "has started to drift decisively away from the rest of the continent. And with every year that passes, the gulf between us is growing wider." Remainers are constantly arguing that Britain's trade depends on Europe. But exports to the rest of the EU peaked in 2006, just before the crash, at 55% of the total, and have been declining ever since.

Indeed, in its latest analysis of the degree and depth of trade within the EU, Eurostat ranks

Britain "right at the very bottom of the table". While the average EU country sells 62% of exports to other union members, the figure for Britain has fallen to 44%. Even allowing for the hiatus of the euro crisis, "a 10 percentage point drop in a decade is a dramatic move, given that trade statistics usually move very slowly". Why has it happened? "Simple. The EU economy has stagnated: GDP is still 6% below what it was in 2008."

There's no point downplaying the importance of Europe to the British economy, says Lynn: 44% is a big chunk of our exports. "But unless you take an extreme view that an impassable trade wall will be built the day after Brexit, then the impact will be marginal."

The bottom line, says Matt Ridley in The Times, is that Britain is locked into a "fortress", which commands a shrinking share of world trade, and is protected by an external tariff that jacks up the prices we pay for imports from non-EU countries.

> Within that fortress there is free trade, but at inflated prices, in things we do not have much comparative advantage in — food and manufactures — and no free trade in the things we do have a comparative advantage in: services. That's why we have a large, and growing trade deficit with the rest of the EU.

Surely, says Ridley, we have a duty to ourselves and future generations to find a deal that fits the particular shape of our economy rather better than that.

The Johnson policy on cake

Of course, in the messy real world there are always barriers to achieving the models dreamt up by economics wonks and free trade crusaders, says Buttonwood in The Economist. Politics, for starters. If we left the EU, would there actually be a majority of Britons who'd favour a full-blooded, no-holds-barred, free-market option? It's hard to imagine Labour, the LibDems or the Greens, let alone the Welsh and Scots Nats, signing up for it. On those grounds alone, the Singapore model might not be realisable.

Then there's the matter of rehashing trade treaties. Outside the EU, Britain would have to replace all 53 of the EU's free-trade pacts from a diminished position of strength. And a post-Brexit Britain would also be excluded from deals with several big countries – including the US, China and India – that the EU is currently negotiating. Could we really hold our own in a world increasingly dominated by large trading blocs and regional trade treaties?

Cutting a preferable Free Trade Agreement with Brussels is also likely to be fraught with difficulty. In his book *The Trouble with Europe,* Roger Bootle of Capital Economics argues that Britain's chances of securing a free trade deal would be boosted by our status as the EU's largest single export market. It certainly isn't hard to imagine every lobby group in Europe – from German car-makers to Italian cheese-makers – converging on Brussels to protest if they were locked out of the UK market. And there's no shortage of alternative models to full EU membership that we might emulate or adapt. The big problem, says The Economist, is that all involve uncomfortable "trade-offs", access to the single market vs the ability to control immigration being the key one.

Brexiters want both. "My policy on cake is pro having it, and pro eating it" is Boris Johnson's line. A delicious idea, but impossible to serve up. Europe's internal market is based on the free movement of goods, capital, services and people; and, under EU law, these "four freedoms" are inseparable. We haven't a clue exactly what negotiating position Brussels might adopt post-Brexit, but we do know that on this point the eurocrats will not budge. To carve up the "four freedoms" would would shake the entire *raison d'être* of the union.

THOSE ALTERNATIVE TRADE MODELS IN FULL

PROS

The Norwegian model

It's been tried and tested – by us. The UK would simply revert to a similar position to the one we held before joining the EU: as a member, like Norway, of the European Free Trade Area (EFTA) enjoying access to the single market via the European Economic Area (EEA) agreement. This rather complicated set-up doesn't appear to have done prosperous Norway any harm.

The Canadian model

The EU's trade deal with Canada is its most ambitious yet and its attempt to reduce regulatory barriers could serve as a model for an even more comprehensive accord with the UK.

The Swiss model

A pick-n-mix approach that might, in theory, work well for Britain. Unlike fellow EFTA members Norway, Iceland and Liechtenstein, Switzerland rejected the EEA Agreement preferring to negotiate bilateral agreements sector by sector. As a result, its courts are largely not bound by EU rulings.

The Turkish model

Turkey is part of the EU's customs union and exports goods to the EU tariff- free, thereby gaining access to the bloc's single market, but bypassing the "four freedoms" that put the stoppers on immigration controls.

CONS

In return for single-market access, Norway has had to accept the EU's "four freedoms" and some other EU laws too – unacceptable to any post-Brexit UK government demanding controls on immigration and a restoration of parliamentary sovereignty. Norway also has to make budget contributions. Yet because it isn't a member of the EU it has no say in decision-making. Arguably the worst of all worlds.

Took ages to negotiate. And although it abolishes tariffs on manufactured goods, it doesn't secure true free trade in financial services – a vital consideration for Britain, given the City's dominance in that sphere.

It would be complicated to negotiate a series of bilateral agreements and the Swiss accords exclude all-important financial services. Furthermore, Switzerland is by no means immune to EU strong-arming: the bloc threatened to cut off market access when the Swiss prepared to cap EU immigration. Under this model we'd still have to contribute to the EU budget.

The deal excludes services and agriculture. Worse, under the rules of this model, Britain wouldn't be able to influence or directly benefit from free trade deals that the EU strikes with many non-EU countries, but would nonetheless have to accept them accessing our own markets.

PROS

The WTO option

"Forget treaties," says Matt Ridley: "almost three-quarters of British trade is already conducted without treaties anyway", under World Trade Organisation rules. And there's no reason why we couldn't do business with the EU on those terms, as do countries like New Zealand. There would be tariffs, but pro-leave campaigners claim that the overall cost of tariffs would be lower than Britain's EU membership fees. Britain would not have to agree to free movement of labour.

UK-tailored deal

Promoters of this solution point to the EU's goods surplus with the UK as an incentive for it to grant UK financial services "equivalence" with EU rivals.

And finally, a new contender...

The Albanian model

This idea, floated by Michael Gove in April, would see Britain move outside the EU's single market – with all the restrictions that entails – and instead join "Bosnia, Serbia, Albania and Ukraine" in a European free-trade zone, stretching from Iceland to the Baltic. All European nations could access it, whether they're in the EU or not. A glorious chance for Britain to lead a pure trade league in Europe as a rebel alternative to the EU.

Sources: Open Europe, The Economist, Financial Times, Newsweek

CONS

Tariffs are low in most sectors but there are exceptions: such as car parts, (one of the UK's leading manufacture exports) agriculture, chemicals and food. Regulatory barriers on financial services would be even more damaging.

The UK already has trouble extracting concessions from the EU. So why would Europe yield to the UK, if it were no longer contributing to the EU budget?

A lot of these countries are actually clamouring to get into the EU. Moreover, Gove's insistence that the City would "continue to thrive" outside the single market – even if financial services firms no longer had "passports" allowing them to operate in the EU – is surely questionable. Is Albania really a suitable model for post-Brexit Britain? The proposition "invites ridicule", and has been "gleefully seized upon by opponents", says the *FT*.

The economy, business and markets

Dodgy dossier?

"There are two possible ways to conduct economic arguments," wrote Allister Heath in The Daily Telegraph in April. "The first is to accept that one's opponents are genuine and intelligent and to attempt to address their arguments as fairly and honestly as possible." The second – the route shamefully taken by the Chancellor in April when he launched his 200-page "dodgy dossier" on the economic impact of a Leave vote – is to heap ridicule on your opponents. George Osborne was guilty of that, and more. His strategy for tackling their arguments was:

> Assume that they are nasty, or stupid or "economically illiterate", before deliberately distorting or ignoring what they have to say while carefully cherry-picking the best possible assumptions to feed into your own mathematical models to generate your favourite conclusions. Forget about trying to be scientific to get at the truth, or having a civil debate: the only thing that matters is winning at any cost.

The Treasury presented "caricatures" of the alternatives to EU membership discussed by eurosceptics, with "no upsides, only supposedly (massive) downsides". It didn't even begin to quantify the gains to be had from EU deregulation, and drew heavily on irrelevant historical scenarios. A key piece of research used to justify the claim that quitting the EU would hit trade (leaving the UK economy 6% smaller by 2030 at a cost equivalent of £4,300 per household) was the impact of the 1967-75 Suez Canal closure. What possible bearing can that have on Brexit and the modern economy?

Besides, the Treasury can't even accurately forecast GDP in the next quarter, so how on earth can it make such confident assumptions about where Britain will be in 2030?

The Remain Camp, of course, took the opposite view. Any report of this kind is bound to be "speculative", pronounced the Financial Times. But the Treasury has nonetheless produced an "authoritative" paper whose conclusions about harmful effects of Brexit accord with "almost every respectable body from the IMF down".

Battleground

The economy was always going to be the principal battleground: the dangers of what the Prime Minister describes as an economic "leap in the dark" aren't difficult to convey to a nation still clawing its way out from the debris of the 2008 crash. For all the *Braveheart* rhetoric that preceded the 2014 Scottish referendum, the economy turned out to be the decisive factor for voters.

"The moment you make a judgement about the impact upon trade of leaving the EU, you are more than halfway to deciding whether you think it is a good idea," says Times columnist Daniel Finkelstein. But the danger is that we lose sight of the bigger picture, says Charles Moore in The Daily Telegraph, which, in this case, is that "trade deals are red herrings". Trade comes from the ground up: formal agreements can help smooth the path, but trade isn't created by politicians and diplomats.

> The EU has never yet in its history had a trade deal with America... Yet trade between the EU and the US, and British trade with America – with whom we have no trade deal – has grown, whereas British trade with the EU, despite the single market, has fallen. Doesn't this suggest that what matters is not any trade agreement, but trade itself?

America and the EU "managed perfectly" well before their current attempt to combine in the "highly controversial" Transatlantic Trade and Investment Partnership. "So would Britain outside the EU."

Flying stats

The problem for voters weighing up these arguments is that the barrage of statistics has shed a good deal more heat than light – and everyone producing them seems to have an axe to grind, a market book to talk up, or a status quo to defend. A report by corporate bean-counters PricewaterhouseCoopers, forecasting that Brexit could cost a million jobs and billions of pounds worth of investment might have carried more weight, noted Private Eye, had PwC not benefited handsomely for decades providing "independent advice to key EU initiatives and programmes". No surprise that it doesn't want the "serious economic shock" of having the trough removed.

"Every investment bank, think-tank and fund manager worth its salt has indicated its views," observed Buttonwood in The Economist. However carefully considered, they tend to get rubbished. When the biggest fund manager in the world, BlackRock, produced an analysis it was immediately accused of being biased because Brexit is bad for fund managers but not for Britain. "Clearly, there is *no* authority that some people will accept."

Who can blame them, given the spread of figures produced? These range from Capital Economics's forecast of "nil" impact on growth, to predictions of a percentage decline even scarier than the Treasury's. Most economists would themselves admit that the "range of variables and scenarios makes the exercise meaningless", said Katie Allen in The Observer. "No accountant or economist can tell voters what trade deals would be negotiated if we voted to leave. Nor can they tell us what immigration rules will be hammered out, which international firms will leave Britain or how UK government bonds will fare in international markets."

The likelihood is that the costs and benefits of Brexit have been exaggerated by both sides, said JP Morgan's chief market strategist, Stephanie Flanders. "We are a successful economy" and if we left "we'd still have a strong trading relationship with Europe, we'd still have attraction to foreign investors".

> The big impact in the short-term would be uncertainties for companies, but this will be a micro uncertainty rather than a macro one because there is no rule that would change overnight. Nothing would happen for two years but every major company would have to think what the cost structure is going to be like, as well as about supply relationships.

Sitting here in limbo

If you believe the statistics, the impact of Brexit is already being felt. "A fog of uncertainty has descended on the corporate sector," noted a Deloitte survey of UK chief financial officers in the run-up to the vote. Decisions on hiring and capital investment have been put on hold, risk appetite is at a three-year low.

The frustration in business circles and the City is palpable. "What really worries me," said the CEO of one FTSE 250 company, "is that this could carry on indefinitely if there's a Leave vote. We could be in a permanent state of limbo while politicians wrangle over deals." It may not matter if corporate numbers are knocked for a couple of quarters – or if the overall UK growth figure is slightly shaved. The worry is the long-term damage that a steady drip of uncertainty could wreak.

The risk of a shock for Britain...

Then there's the financial tumult that Brexit could cause. In February, Boris Johnson threw his weight behind the Out campaign – prompting the pound to suffer one of its worst days since the financial crisis. If the defection of one "plummy-voiced, crazily coiffed, media-darling career politician" can cause the pound to drop 2%, what, wondered Katie Martin in the FT, would be the fall-out from full-scale Brexit?

Predictions range from carnage (Goldman Sachs reckons sterling would plunge 25%), to the nonchalant view that a weaker pound would be big plus for Britain's exporters after a long period of currency strength. Yet even the most ardent Brexiteers concede that short-term ructions are inevitable.

Britain's chief problem, as the Bank of England governor, Mark Carney, has pointed out, is that we are more reliant than ever "on the kindness of strangers". The UK's current account deficit – the difference between what the nation pays and earns abroad – is at its widest since World War Two. For the moment, global investors seem happy to finance it, but the deficit makes Britain much more vulnerable to any loss of international confidence. Brexit could trigger a shock, with a deep devaluation of sterling and a consequent precipitous rise in interest rates. And markets are clearly worried. The cost of buying insurance against a plunge in the pound has risen to its highest level since the scary days of 2008. Grounds for concern, wherever you stand on the vote.

...and for Europe

Much of the economic debate has focused on "an assumption that it is the UK that has most to gain or lose" from Brexit, says Simon Nixon in The Wall Street Journal. That may be misplaced. The greatest impact could be felt on the continent. Deutsche Bank considers the threat so serious that in January its chief economist, David Folkerts-Landau, warned that the "devastating" effect of

Brexit could relegate the EU to the status of a "second-rate" world power. Even in the most benign scenario, argues Nixon,

> the eurozone economy is bound to suffer from a breach with its largest trading partner. At the very least, uncertainty over the political response [to a No vote] is likely to trigger increased risk aversion in markets, causing bonds and equities to sell off [and] a tightening of financial conditions.

That could cause havoc in a continent whose central bank is already stretched to capacity pumping out cash in a massive quantitative easing programme, raising questions about whether the ECB would have enough ammunition to deal with another shock. All the more so since – in a bad coincidence of timing – there's another Greek debt cliff-hanger looming this summer. The Brexit and Grexit risks "could clash horribly", says Hugo Dixon on Reuters Breakingviews. Given multiple troubles on other fronts, that would spell trouble for a fragile world economy.

Brexit could well deliver "a profound geopolitical shock" that would reignite doubts about the future of the single currency and lead to further political fragmentation in many countries, concludes Nixon. The risk is of a repeat of the "vicious spiral" of the eurozone debt crisis. Ironically, "the UK might even come to be seen as a safe haven". But given the wider economic and financial fall-out likely from another implosion in the eurozone that should be no consolation. And we tend to underestimate the risk. "Project Fear? Not yet fearful enough."

Reform or skidaddle?

Some in business have predicted a return to the virtual dark ages if Britain votes to leave. But what about the dangers of voting to remain? If we believe Sunday Telegraph columnist Simon Heffer, the truly scary economic threat is of staying shackled to what he dismisses as "a group of underachievers with a malfunctioning currency union that is heading for the rocks". Heffer cites research by economist Dr Savvas Savouri of the London-based hedge fund ToscaFund, who argues that the Brussels machine has become so "frustratingly technocratic and bureaucratic" that its declining clout on the world stage is matched only by its internal scleroticism: witness the "deteriorating economic fortunes across the EU". Our choice is clear, says Heffer: it is "between decline and ambition".

Even if you don't share the arch-pessimism about Europe's future, it's hard to find any commentator who doesn't view the eurozone's inherent economic contradictions as a continuing drag on growth that could yet spark break-up. As the former Bank of England governor, Mervyn

King, puts it in *The End of Alchemy*: "Eventually the choice between a return to national monies and democratic control, or a clear and abrupt transfer of political sovereignty to a European government, cannot be avoided."

When you add up all the problems that Europe faces – the chaos over Schengen, the failure of the European Central Bank's monetary policy, the probable solvency problems of both the eurozone's big banks and its big countries (France and Italy being the obvious candidates) – "you must accept that it is likely the eurozone will see an existential crisis in the next few years", says Merryn Somerset Webb in the Financial Times. Why risk getting caught in the deluge? "As the Brexiteers say, better to watch from a comfortable lifeboat in the Channel." Any initial turbulence is a price worth paying to avoid total shipwreck.

Yet even assuming that the EU really is destined for long-term economic decline, Britain already has a proven means of making a nimble escape. Our existing semi-detached relationship – most important-antly the retention of the pound – protected us from the worst of the 2012 debt crisis and would surely offer protection again should the bloc implode.

Should the opposite evil – greater political integration – threaten, we also have protection of sorts. The reform package hammered out by David Cameron with other EU leaders in February included a financial stability provision to safeguard Britain's future outside the eurozone. "I would not like to rely on it in a dark night," said Andrew Tyrie, chairman of the Commons Treasury Select Committee. But Mark Carney has professed himself satisfied.

> The settlement explicitly recognises the needs of the UK to supervise its financial stability, while not impeding the implementation of necessary, further integration among members of the euro area. It recognises that there is more than one currency in the EU and makes a legally-binding commitment to ensure non-discrimination in the single market on the basis of currency.

Some Brexiters, including Capital Economics's Roger Bootle, argue that disintegration might be the best, indeed possibly the only way, to revitalise European economies. But those campaigning for reform within the EU, such as the former Greek finance minister Yanis Varoufakis, urge Britain to fight for it from within.

> If Britain comes out, at some point a major fault-line will develop down the Rhine and across the Alps. Germany is going to simply create a new Deutsche Mark zone with Netherlands, Poland, the Czechs, Slovakia and the Baltics... In that environment, Britain is going to suffer even if it's out of the European Union. There will be a black hole in Europe [and] Britain will be sucked in.

Whichever way the UK votes in June, the future of

the EU already hangs in the balance: events could move either way. Writing in the FT in March, Wolfgang Munchau bemoaned the Remain camp's lack of passion: all the arguments for staying were "pragmatic". Yet centuries of British involvement on the continent has surely taught us that keeping our options open has served us well. From an economic perspective, at least, you might consider that the British are best off where we already are: sitting on the fence.

A close shave

A vivid – and not necessarily welcome – image seared into the minds of a certain generation of Britons is that of Norman Lamont sitting in his bath singing the Edith Piaf song *Je Ne Regrette Rien*. At the time, in 1992, Lamont's apparent lack of contrition was thought outrageous. The Tory Chancellor had just presided over a financial earthquake: he had failed to prevent Britain crashing out of the Exchange Rate Mechanism, the precursor to our planned entry into the euro.

Contemporary news reports highlight just what a shock "Black Wednesday" (September 19th 1992) was. David Cameron, an aide to Lamont at the time, can doubtless confirm it. A "tidal wave" of speculators selling the pound on foreign exchanges "left sterling defenceless", reported Larry Elliott in The Guardian. At the end of a day of "desperate and futile attempts" to prop up the pound – including raising interest rates twice and spending £10bn of Britain's reserves – Lamont announced "the Government could no longer hold the line". The episode marked a "humiliating reversal" for the Chancellor and the PM, John Major, "who have staked enormous credibility on being able to resist devaluation", observed Elliott. Indeed the following spring, Lamont was sacked from the Treasury. The two men didn't speak to each for over a decade.

The immediate result of this "farce" was "a massive transfer of wealth to the billionaire specu-lator George Soros", who became known as "the man who broke the Bank of England", recalls Neil Collins in The Spectator. Less remarked upon at the time was the impact of being freed from a mechanism designed "to make our economy more like Germany's": thousands of UK companies suddenly became competitive, contributing to a rebound in the economy "that allowed Gordon Brown to claim with a straight face eight years later that he had abolished boom and bust".

Nonetheless, it took the long drawn out crash of the eurozone debt crisis to ram home to most Britons just what a close shave we'd had. Thanks to the Black Wednesday debacle, the UK largely stayed out of the fray. Meanwhile, we continue to benefit from what Soros now describes as "the best of both worlds": attracting foreign investment from elsewhere in the world because of our access to the single market, while retaining control of our own currency.

Eurosceptics, Lamont now included, take a different line. For them, the enduring lesson of Black Wednesday is the challenge it poses to the claim that leaving the EU would be ruinous for Britain. All the "experts" were agreed upon that in 1992 – and look what happened.

Sovereignty – who governs?

The most basic test of a functioning democracy, the late Labour left-winger Tony Benn used to say, can be boiled down to two questions: "Who elected you? And how can we get rid of you?"

Central to the Brexit case is that the European Commission – the body that governs the EU and legislates for it – fails on both counts. True, the European Parliament, which *is* directly elected by voters, has powers to amend and block EU laws. MEPs are also tasked with approving the appointment of Commissioners and are the only people who can sack them. But in practice what does this mean? It takes a near earthquake to shake Brussels's entrenched institutions. Indeed, MEPs have only really rebelled once – in 1999, when the entire Commission, led by Jacques Santer, resigned following accusations of fraud, mismanagement and cronyism.

"No one can deny that the EU's government, the

Commission, is unelected and cannot be removed by any of us through elections," argues the Labour MP, Kate Hoey. "That fact alone is enough to reject the EU" – it is "anti-democratic".

> At least when I oppose Tory policies, I can vote on them. We can't do this with the EU. It is an attempt to replace the democratic power of the people with a permanent administration in the interests of big business. Everything else is a smokescreen.

Hoey's view of the EU may differ in some respects from that of eurosceptic Tories, but they agree with her about Brussels's lack of accountability. "If we vote to stay, we're not settling for a secure status quo," says the Justice Secretary, Michael Gove.

> We're voting to be hostages locked in the back of the car and driven headlong towards deeper EU integration.... We're a uniquely inventive nation. Our greatest invention is representative democracy – the principle that the people who run our country should be chosen by us and can be kicked out by us. It's time to take back control.

For Boris Johnson, the final straw was when Whitehall lawyers rejected his submission of new wording to assert the sovereignty of Parliament and of British courts over EU institutions, ahead of David Cameron's February renegotiation.

German Chancellor Angela Merkel with David Cameron at the Chancellery in Berlin

"The government lawyers... just blew up," Johnson told the BBC's Andrew Marr. "They said: 'basically this voids our obligations under the 1972 European Communities Act [which implicitly recognises the primacy of EU law over British law]. It doesn't work. We can't.'"

So much for the oft-repeated claim that Britain voted to stay in a simple trading community in the 1975 referendum.

Political graveyard?

The trouble is that most of us have no clue as to how the Brussels power structure works, or who's in charge. If the EU is the faceless monolith of popular repute, it's partly because we've made it that way. We can't be bothered really. When was the last time you voted in a European election?

Most of us see Brussels either as a gravy train or a graveyard for politicians we've grown tired of. As the "make me redundant" MEP, Dan Hannan, observes, there's surely a horrible irony in this.

> We fought a civil war in this country to establish the principle that laws should not be passed, nor taxes raised, except by our own elected representatives. And now supreme power is held by people who tend to owe their positions to having just LOST elections: Peter Mandelson, Neil Kinnock, and what have you.

To defenders of Europe this is churlish. After all, the most important founding purpose of the EU – even in its early economic community days – was to safeguard European democracy and peace. Many of the founders lived under and fought fascism. During the campaign, however, Michael Gove urged Britons to rise up and lose their chains – and encouraged other European nations to do likewise. The EU may have *once* been "a beacon" of freedom for countries wanting to leave their totalitarian pasts behind, he said. "It was the case that to enter the EU you had to prove that you adhered to certain democratic principles." But that's no longer true: those principles have steadily been eroded by the organisation itself.

Does sovereignty actually matter?

Writing in The Daily Telegraph, Allister Heath (a Briton raised in France) contrasted his philosophy-rich education there to the thin gruel served up in the British system. Maybe if we knew a little more about the history of political thought and concepts of sovereignty, he argued, we'd have a better idea about the dangers posed by the EU, and its supporters' Rousseau-esque idea that we need to be guided by "an enlightened elite". In reality, Heath added, that means "rule by a transnational *nomenklatura*".

The media is partly to blame for the lack – until recently, at least – of any serious national debate about sovereignty, maintains the former Downing Street spin doctor, Alistair Campbell, who remembers constantly rebutting stories that

> bent bananas and cucumbers were going to be banned; the British army was going to vanish; Cheddar cheese and Scotch whisky were going to have to be renamed; lollipop ladies were to be outlawed; we were going to have to drive on the right... some Luxembourg or Belgian nonentity was going to replace the Queen.

Perhaps that's the point about sovereignty. Classically-educated politicians get agitated about abstruse points of democratic theory and sovereignty. And people love grumbling about EU idiocies. But do most of us really care?

Besides, when we consider what the EU has actually contributed to our daily lives, haven't the effects been more beneficial than otherwise? Leave supporters argue that cleaner beaches, improved consumer and employee protections, and equality and human rights legislation would have happened in Britain anyway. Yet there's no doubt that having the weight of the Brussels machine behind them hastened the process. What's more, when we really don't like something the eurocrats have cooked up, aren't we actually rather good at securing exemptions? That's certainly the view of our EU partners, often exasperated by what they consider to be Britain's "special pleading" and stubborn wiliness in negotiations.

The myth of sovereignty

It is often asserted these days that "sovereignty is a myth", writes Clive Crook on Bloomberg: that "the very idea of self-government" in a middle-sized country like Britain "is mostly a delusion". Outside the union, "Britain's government would still be constrained by the forces of geopolitics and economics". What rot, says Crook. To take a North American example:

> Does Canada have more actually useful
> sovereignty than, say, California? Of course.

When Canada writes its laws, it's constrained by economics, geopolitics and heaven knows what else, but it's still in charge of writing its laws. Where trade-offs must be struck, Canada chooses how to strike them.

Some maintain, however, that, even within Britain, the Westminster model of sovereignty has already "had its day" – and "external factors like EU membership are only partly to blame". Britain's constitutional tradition, forged in the late 19th century, is based on the institution of Parliament as the "absolute 'sovereign' lawmaker", write Dr Jo Eric Khushal Murkens and Dr Simon Toubeau in a London School of Economics paper. But it isn't any more. Moreover, the greatest "losses" to Westminster's sovereignty stem from "domestic developments" – notably the fragmentation of the old two-party system, the emergence of devolved governments in Scotland, Wales and Northern Ireland, and increased power-sharing with the regions.

Since the UK is itself "more federal", we might as well put the experience to good use, they conclude. "The rising practice of power-sharing" within Britain should "inform the UK's relationship with the EU".

But to everyone in the Out camp, "power-sharing" the EU way is really about forfeiting control of our destiny – and ceding important freedoms.

Who makes our laws?

As things stand currently, how much legislative power has the UK actually ceded to the EU? As ever, it's hard to find a definitive answer. Business for Britain, which campaigns under the Leave umbrella, says more than 60% of UK law is influenced by EU law. But that figure may be exaggerated. When Clive Coleman investigated for the BBC's Newsnight, he found that, between 1993 and 2014, Parliament passed 945 Acts of which 231 implemented EU obligations of some sort. During the same period, Parliament also passed 33,160 "statutory instruments" (which flesh out how a statute will work), 4,283 of which implemented EU obligations.

PUNCHING OUR WEIGHT

Not only do our interests increasingly differ from those of eurozone members but, while never "at the heart of Europe"... we are now becoming increasingly marginalised as we are doomed to being consistently outvoted by the eurozone bloc.

Nigel Lawson's opinion (expressed in 2013) sums up a constant anxiety in Britain – that we frequently come off worse in EU decision-making. Is he right?

The man to ask is Simon Hix, professor of political science at the London School of Economics, who is also a prime mover in the non-partisan "UK in a Changing Europe" research unit. He's sifted through the data of voting decisions made across the EU institutions to find whether there's any evidence of "marginalisation".

Hix took as his starting

When you crunch the numbers, says Coleman, it turns out that about 13% of UK laws during the period were influenced by the EU. But that low figure is misleading because most EU regulations "don't need laws to bring them into effect". Once you include those, the Business for Britain figure suddenly looks more convincing. "If you count all EU regulation, EU-related Acts of Parliament and EU-related statutory instruments, about 62% of laws introduced between 1993 and 2014 implement EU obligations."

Of course, as Coleman points out, just adding these up isn't that useful. "The Working Time Directive, which gives workers a minimum number of holidays and rest breaks is pretty significant. The

point a data set put together by Prof Robert Thomson of Strathclyde University which looked at 125 pieces of legislation between 1996 and 2008. In that period, he found little evidence that Britain wasn't punching its weight. On the contrary, we did rather well when our policy preferences were matched to final outcomes – on average coming in as "the fourth closest (i.e. most effective) actor". "The results are even more positive from a UK perspective" on issues we really cared about, where Britain was the second top performer (after Greece!), doing better than any other large member state.

Breaking down the legislation by policy area, final outcomes were close to UK positions on tax, social affairs, justice, home affairs, transport, fisheries and migration. We didn't, however, do so well on internal market issues (including financial services regulation), agriculture and trade.

A lot of water has gone under the bridge since 2008. But in the period studied there was little evidence of British "marginalisation". ∎

regulations classifying padded waistcoats in things like Puffa jackets, less so" (unless, a Brexiteer might point out, you happen to make them). Moreover, quitting the EU wouldn't actually free us from its regulations anyway. If we want to sell into the single market, we'd have to produce goods that comply with EU rules.

Given the weight of European influence on British laws and regulation, it's perhaps understandable that a key issue of the debate is how far Britain is "marginalised" in EU decision-making. According to the Labour MP, Chuka Umunna:

> It's just not true that we get trampled on in the EU. Nine out of ten times, we're on the majority side. If you want control, don't give it up by sacrificing your power of influence... As for sovereignty, if you took the Leave campaigners' argument, the most sovereign nation in the world would probably be North Korea – because they don't work with anyone.

Who controls our justice system?

Soon after Britain joined the EU in 1973, the presiding Master of the Rolls, the great "people's judge" Lord Denning, compared the legal consequences to "an incoming tide" that "flows into the estuaries and up the rivers".

At first sight, however, the powers of Europe's

two highest courts – the Luxembourg-based European Court of Justice and the European Court of Human Rights in Strasbourg – look containable. Formally, neither can overrule the UK Supreme Court (UKSC), which took over from the law lords in the House of Lords as the highest appeal court in the land in 2009. But there are limits to that independence. When making decisions, the UKSC has to "give effect", in the jargon, to the rights contained in the European Convention of Human Rights (ECHR), as contained in the Human Rights Act of 1998. It must also give effect to directly applicable EU law, and interpret domestic law consistently with EU law "so far as is possible".

What particularly exercises legally-minded Leave campaigners, though, is the fact that the two pan-European courts can, if they choose, effectively overrule the decisions of the UK Parliament. As Britain's most senior judge, Supreme Court president Lord Neuberger, observed in 2014, that is "little short of offensive to our notions of constitutional propriety".

"The flow of legal ideas and concepts between Britain and mainland Europe" has always been a two-way process, Neuberger argued: much of England's common law tradition was derived from Norman imports. "Yet the notion that it is unacceptable for 'unelected judges to impose a diktat' on a democratically elected parliament, is peculiarly British." The UK has no history of courts overruling parliament, and the idea is particularly inflammatory if "the courts concerned are not even British courts".

Reaching a verdict

It's hard to gainsay the argument that Britain has ceded a good deal of sovereignty to Europe, and that Michael Gove is probably right when he says that we lose a little more each day. The question is: does it matter?

Gove was widely mocked by Remainers when he evoked William Pitt the Younger during the campaign: "If we vote to leave we will have... saved our country by our exertions and Europe by our example."

The danger, said Labour's down-to-earth former postie, Alan Johnson, is that we chuck away a valuable relationship – from which Britain has already gained a great deal – to "walk off into something that we now understand is a bit of Michael Gove rhetoric".

On the other hand, the issues that Gove highlights are arguably fundamental to core notions of what Britain is and the values it stands for. The lack of democratic accountability in the EU as presently structured – with its "central bureaucracy" and "mock parliament" – is not only injurious to British notions of freedom and justice, but poses a direct threat to political stability. Without direct accountability, Gove says, what you end up with is "confusion, corruption and cynicism".

> When people ask why is there an anti-politics mood in this country – why is it that in other EU countries people are voting out of frustration for parties on the fringes that peddle simplistic solutions – the answer is that politicians themselves have acquiesced in a process where they give up control, they give up accountability, they give up democracy.

This contest, as often been observed, shouldn't be decided by arithmetic alone. You've got to draw a line somewhere. Maybe by staying within the EU fold, we are quietly selling our collective soul.

Fortress Britain: immigration, borders and security

Last year, the richest Pole in Britain, Prince Jan Żyliński, challenged Nigel Farage to a duel with swords in Hyde Park. The elderly aristocrat said he was fed up with the witch hunt that the Ukip leader had been conducting against Polish workers in Britain and wanted to make a "symbolic and visual" protest. Sadly, Farage said no. But the point was made, says Bartosz Wieliński of the Warsaw newspaper Gazeta Wyborcza. Poles in Britain don't like being branded as benefits scroungers by a country where they live, work and pay tax.

Benefits gained... and benefits paid

European nationals don't need a visa to enter Britain because of the EU's fundamental right of free movement. And it is true that the number of European workers living in Britain has risen sharply. According to Capital Economics, annual net migration from Europe has more than doubled since 2012, reaching 183,000 in March 2015. A good many of the incomers are Poles. According to data from the Office for National Statistics, Polish nationals were the largest non-British community in the UK in 2013, with an estimated 726,000 living here.

Boris Johnson accused the PM David Cameron of achieving "two thirds of diddly squat" in his pre-referendum negotiations with Brussels. That's certainly a widespread view among voters worried about the impact of immigration on the welfare system – particularly since the best concession that Cameron could extract from his February re-negotiation with the EU was a watered-down version of his initial proposal for a four-year ban on in-work benefits for EU migrants, and the promise of an "emergency brake" if the strain on public services becomes overwhelming.

But a number of "respected studies" show that, far from sapping the country, migration from the European Union is a net positive for the Exchequer, says economist Simon French of Panmure Gordon, "in sharp contrast with the contribution of the domestic-born population and migrants from outside the EU". French concludes that any future government looking to limit migration flows risks "damaging the positive contribution that EU migrants currently provide".

It's often lost in the wider debate just how important immigration has been to Britain's economy. One reason why UK growth has out-performed that of continental Europe in recent years is that we have a younger population – and that is mainly down to the force of newcomers. "Britain's demographics are the best of any of the 28 EU states, save Ireland," notes the serial entre-preneur Luke Johnson. "As they say, over time, demographics is destiny."

The Australian dream

Many British businesses have benefited from the availability of European workers – as has a re-covering UK economy. Capital Economics points out that cheap labour has "helped support the economy's ability to grow without pushing up wage growth and inflation, keeping interest rates lower for longer". But if you visit the Leave.eu website and read the testimonials posted by many small traders, it becomes swiftly apparent how resentful (and out-of-pocket) many feel.

What Nigel Farage would like to see is more "targeted" immigration, along the lines of the Australian points-based system. To come to Australia, you must be under 45 and have a skill or trade that will bring a benefit to the country.

> What they say is we don't care whether you're black or white or yellow, or what your religion is. But if you come to our country to take citizenship, you become part of us and you become part of our Australian dream. That is exactly what we should be doing.

"Permitting uncontrolled entry of unskilled immigrants from the EU, while heavily restricting immigration of skilled labour from elsewhere, makes bad policy," agrees Luke Johnson in The Guardian. Prioritising EU immigration has costs if it means the doors are shut to hiring a red-hot IT genius from Hyderabad, or promoting a talented Brazilian executive to the London HQ. Economies and people are infinitely adaptable, as anecdotes of eastern European workers being taught how to cook chicken tikka masala because of a shortage of Asian chefs illustrate. But many companies make no bones about their frustration with the system.

Man the borders

The influx from Europe has undoubtedly put pressure on an already stretched NHS and education system, as well as exacerbating Britain's chronic shortage of housing. You can hear as much on the streets. "We should definitely come out," one Romford shopper told The Guardian. "We're overcrowded as it is. We've got no houses for our own children. You go down the hospital and you're waiting hours. You've got old people left on trolleys."

Distressing scenes of refugees attempting desperate Mediterranean crossings, or being holed up in appalling conditions in Calais, touched consciences but didn't alter the general view. "It sounds like we're being horrible. Those poor people – if it was us, we would want to get to somewhere better. But you can't just keep taking them."

Why, ask Ukippers, should Britain have to accommodate the German Chancellor Angela Merkel's unilateral decision last year to open Germany's borders to all-comers? There's a widespread view that Merkel "turned a manageable refugee crisis into an unmanageable one", says the FT's Wolfgang Munchau. The entry of 1.2 million "irregular migrants" into the bloc last year very nearly saw the suspension of the Schengen agreement – a central pillar of the EU which guarantees passport-free travel across most of the union (but not to Britain which opted out). It might yet happen. In December, EU ministers discussed suspending the Schengen zone for two years on the basis that "serious deficiencies" at the Greek border could endanger the whole of the bloc. It underlines how gravely the EU's integration project has been threatened.

It's a standard rallying cry of the Leave camp that if Britain left the EU we could take back "control of our borders". In fact, the chances of that are unlikely – unless we took the radical decision to quit the European single market altogether. Non-EU countries like Norway and Switzerland actually have higher levels of European immigration than Britain. The think-tank, Open Europe, notes that in 2013 Norway was the destination of twice as many migrants per head as the UK. In Switzerland in 2013 15.6% of citizens were born in EU countries, compared with only 4.2% of British citizens.

Closing our borders could also have unintended effects within the British Isles, as The Economist's Buttonwood columnist points out.

It is worth thinking about what control of immigration would mean for Ireland. The Northern Ireland/Ireland border is now open; people move freely across it. All EU citizens have the right to move to Ireland, so any attempt to control their movement would require border controls between NI and the rest of Ireland. Were Scotland to leave the UK, as it might in the event of a Brexit vote, there would have to be border controls at Carlisle and Berwick as well. Does that seem unthinkable? If it does, then it is tough to see how the UK would have control of its borders.

Freedom for criminals and terrorists?

Matthew Elliott, one of the leaders of the Vote Leave campaign, has argued that free movement of people in Europe puts "British families in danger". To illustrate the point, he published a list of serious criminals from other member states who have been allowed into Britain.

But because of our opt-out from Schengen, it was not freedom of movement that allowed the criminals in, but the deficiencies of the UK Border Agency, says Chris Giles in the FT. European law allows Britain to refuse entry to people "on grounds of public policy, public security or public health" – and that has been translated into guidelines for officials. It's not the EU's fault if they didn't follow them. Surely "the more important point is that a lack of co-operation between EU states can prevent UK officials from knowing about the criminal past of people entering the country".

There is a similar argument about terrorist suspects. Brexiters seized on the pronouncement, from a former head of Interpol, that "the current EU system is like hanging a sign welcoming terrorists to Britain", because the EU sets the bar for taking meaningful action impossibly high.

Then the former head of MI6, Sir Richard

Dearlove, stepped in, writing in Prospect magazine:

> Brexit would bring two potentially important security gains: the ability to dump the European Convention on Human Rights – remember the difficulty of extraditing the extremist Abu Hamza of the Finsbury Park Mosque – and, more importantly, greater control over immigration from the European Union.

What's more, argued Dearlove, the idea that the UK has much to gain from the EU's intelligence efforts is nonsense. "Britain is Europe's leader in intelligence and security matters and gives much more than it gets in return." Politicians talk "loosely" about intelligence sharing, but intelligence sources have to be protected – and, given the "vastly varying levels of professionalism in intelligence and security" between EU member states, "the larger powers cannot put their best intelligence in such colanders". As for the idea that Brexit would damage our far more important defence and intelligence relationship with the US, "I conclude confidently that no, it would not".

Indeed, the one area of the debate that most commentators are agreed upon is that, whatever the outcome of the referendum, Britain's defence interests will remain, in Dearlove's words "firmly hitched to Nato".

The first duty of any government is to protect its citizens. And whether Britain stays in or out of the

EU, we need to build up our intelligence networks on the continent to tackle the international web of Isis cells, argued Niall Ferguson in The Sunday Times. Europol, the EU's law enforcement agency may be "underfunded and over-stretched", but it is at least a beginning.

Conclusion

In February, when Clive Crook penned his excellent analysis of the Brexit debate, *Britain's Unsolvable Problem with Europe*, his conclusion was evident in the title. The country is "stuck in a loveless marriage," he wrote. Staying in Europe will mean very difficult compromises for Britain, which probably "won't ever feel it belongs". Yet the odds are stacked against a successful Brexit.

> If a friendly divorce were feasible, and if the other short term risks weren't so great, I'd vote to quit... But I fear it is too late. Britain lacks a better alternative... Sad, but there you are. Britain chose to get hitched a long time ago and some decisions just have to be lived with.

Yet for a large number of voters, the decision to stay in the union is much more than just an uncomfortable trade-off. It is a hopeful vote for a collective future with our fellow Europeans – and, by the same token, a rejection of xenophobia, prejudice and reactionary Little Englandism. The EU is far from ideally structured in its present state. But which political institution ever began life perfectly? If it doesn't work, we must make it work.

Much has been written about the breakdown of the voters, between cities and the shires, say. But for The Times's Janice Turner the salient divide is between "the prescience of youth" and "wise old age".

> The young talk of open borders: the old wonder how nations will collect tax. The old know that before empires fall, they over-expand. They hear young people hail as progressive an unaccountable bureaucracy that makes British fishermen chuck their catch in landfill and suppresses wages and they laugh... From my Janus-headed middle age, the old look stubborn, the young seem shallow fools. Neither has a monopoly on truth.

Indeed, well into the campaign, it's striking how little entrenched ideological positions have shifted. Diehards on either side find it hard to believe how the other camp can be quite so blind. One person's lethal act of self-sabotage is another's necessary break for freedom.

A hypothetical question often aired is where Churchill would have stood in the debate. Asking the question isn't just nostalgic whimsy. The wartime leader has his critics, but his views are relevant. Churchill spent much of his lengthy political life pondering the question of Britain's relationship with Europe – and seems to have been just as torn about it as many of us.

He first wrote about the possibility of a "United States of Europe" in 1930, inspired by a tour he'd made of the US where he was struck by how the single market had helped economic growth.

Later, after World War Two, Churchill made a series of inspiring speeches arguing that future peace and prosperity depended on a unified Europe. "The whole movement of the world is towards an interdependence of nations. We feel all around us that it is our best hope," he said in 1950. Churchill's grandson, the MP Nicholas Soames, is in no doubt his grandfather was a "profound believer in the values of European co-operation". And the Churchill of the Tehran, Yalta and Potsdam conferences would never have doubted the importance of having a seat at table. The same view is taken across much of Europe, where Churchill is held up as a founding "father" of the union.

In possibly his most famous quote on the subject, however, Churchill had no problem telling President Charles de Gaulle where he drew the line.

"Get this quite clear. Every time we have to decide between Europe and the open sea, it is always the open sea we shall choose."

In his 2014 book, *The Churchill Factor,* Boris Johnson argues that Churchill certainly had a vision of a united Europe, but that the weight of evidence suggests that he saw Britain as "somehow dwelling apart" – associated *with* it, but not of it.

The natural response of those who accuse the London mayor of hitching a ride on Churchill's coat-tails is that he would say that, wouldn't he? The same is probably true of Johnson's assessment that Churchill's defining strength as a politician was his ability to bounce back from a long list of debacles.

Any one of those fiascos on its own would have permanently disabled a normal politician. That Churchill kept going at all is a tribute to his bounce-back-ability, to some Kevlar substance with which he insulated his ego and his morale.

Having loped through 60 years of British history in this book, it's possible to make the same case for Britain's own "bounce-back-ability" as Johnson makes for Churchill's. Whichever course we take, there is always the chance of disaster. Yet the likelihood is that the country will probably muddle through. We always do. Whichever way you eventually vote on June 23rd, do it in a spirit of optimism.

A SHORT HISTORY OF THE EU – AND BRITAIN'S INVOLVEMENT WITH IT

1951: Formation of the European Coal and Steel Community. Six countries join: France, Germany, Belgium, the Netherlands, Luxembourg and Italy. The plan is to pool production as part of the post-WWII reconstruction effort.

1957: The Treaty of Rome establishes the European Economic Community (EEC) to create a common market and a customs union between the six founding nations. Britain declines to join.

1958: European Court of Justice formed to interpret the Treaty of Rome and rule on disputes.

1963: Britain's application to join the EEC, championed by the Conservative PM Harold MacMillan, is vetoed by French President Charles de Gaulle.

1967: De Gaulle vetoes again.

1971: The Conservative PM, Edward Heath, announces his intention to apply for a third time.

1972: Parliament passes the European Communities Act, implicitly recognising the primacy of EU law over UK law.

1973: Heath leads Britain into the EEC (aka the Common Market). Ireland and Denmark also join.

1974: The Labour leader, Harold Wilson, pledges a referendum in Labour's general election manifesto, following a sustained anti-EEC campaign from the left and the trade unions.

1975: Referendum. A resounding 67% of Britons vote to stay in the Common Market.

1979: The launch of the Ecu, a pan-European currency unit. An Exchange Rate Mechanism (ERM) is formed to determine exchange-rate bands with national currencies. All EC members join except Britain.

1981: Greece becomes the EC's 10th member.

1984: The Tory PM, Margaret Thatcher, wields her handbag, negotiating a permanent UK rebate on EC contributions because Britain receives less in agricultural subsidies than other countries.

1985: The new president of the European Commission, Jacques Delors, starts pushing for greater integration. He proposes the creation of a "single market" by 1992, eliminating remaining barriers to free trade and capital and labour movement.

1986: The Single European Act boosts the legislative powers of the European Parliament, marking the first commitment to create a "European Union". Portugal and Spain join. There are now 12 stars on the new blue European Flag.

1988: Margaret Thatcher makes a keynote speech in Bruges rejecting Delors' "European superstate". Bruges becomes the rallying cry of a growing cabal of eurosceptic Tory MPs.

1990: A celebrated Sun headline – Up Yours Delors – urges readers to tell that "French fool where to stuff his Ecu". Nonetheless, Britain enters the Exchange Rate Mechanism.

1992, February: The new Tory leader, John Major, signs The Maastricht Treaty, creating the European Union, a single market, and a single currency: the euro. Britain secures opt-outs from the euro and the "Social Chapter" enabling Brussels to impose directives on working practices, health & safety and equality. Critics slam the treaty as a surrender of sovereignty. Rebels in the Cabinet – dubbed the "Bastards" by Major – call for a confidence vote on the PM's handling of the treaty.

1992 September: "Black Wednesday". With sterling under mounting pressure in markets, the Chancellor, Norman Lamont, announces Britain's withdrawal from the ERM.

1993: The UK Independence Party (Ukip) founded.

1995: Austria, Finland and Sweden join the EU, bringing membership to 15. Britain declines to join the Schengen Agreement which sees seven member states lift border controls.

1997: The new Labour PM, Tony Blair signs the Social Chapter and pushes for Britain to join the euro. The more sceptical Chancellor, Gordon Brown, puts the plans on hold.

1998: Establishment of European Central Bank.

1999: The entire European Commission, led by Jacques Santer, resigns following accusations of fraud, mismanagement and cronyism.

2002: Euro notes and coins enter circulation in the 12 participating states of the new "eurozone".

2004: Ten new countries join: Cyprus, the Czech Republic, Estonia, Hungary, Latvia, Lithuania, Malta, Poland, the Slovak Republic, and Slovenia.

2007: Bulgaria and Romania join, bringing EU membership to 27. The controversial Treaty of Lisbon hands further powers to Brussels.

2011: The new Conservative PM, David Cameron promises to bring back powers from Brussels. After failing to gain exemptions, he uses Britain's veto to block a new treaty setting new budget rules. Other European leaders accuse Britain of putting its own interests ahead of solving the EU's ongoing sovereign debt crisis.

2013: Cameron promises an EU referendum if the Conservatives win the next election. Polls suggest Ukip support stands at 10%. Croatia joins the EU.

2015: The Schengen open borders agreement comes under threat amid a mounting immigration crisis. As Cameron sets out to secure EU reforms, the "British Question" is an unwelcome distraction for many European leaders.

2016: Cameron secures a package of reforms – including an exemption from "ever closer union" and amendments to migrant benefits, but sceptics dismiss them as inconsequential. The referendum date is set for June 23rd.

GLOSSARY

Acquis communautaire: the entire body of European laws, including all treaties, regulations and directives – and the rulings of the European Court of Justice.

Common Agriculture Policy (CAP): The CAP's system of agricultural subsidies was crucial to Europe's recovery after the war, but it swiftly led to over-production – hence the EU's famous "butter mountains" and "wine lakes", and the subsequent "set aside" policy that rewarded farmers for leaving arable land fallow. Critics argue that the CAP has kept Europe's food prices artificially high, while damaging farmers elsewhere in the world (by making it hard for them to compete).

The CAP is also ruinously expensive, though not quite as expensive as it once was. In 1970 it absorbed a staggering 87% of the EU budget in 1970; now it's around 40% (amounting to E57.5bn in 2013). But most of this money still goes in direct subsidies to farmers. And there are many more of them: the eastern enlargement of 2004-07 increased the EU's agricultural land by 40%, adding seven million farmers to the existing six million.

Who benefits most? A 2013 BBC analysis found that farmers in the 15 older EU member states did better than newer members: France, the biggest producer, got 17% of CAP payments, followed by Spain (13%), Germany (12%), Italy (10.6%) and the UK (7%). The average annual subsidy per farm was E12,200. But the main beneficiaries of CAP remain large agri-businesses and big landowners. In 2013, about 80% of farm aid went to a quarter of EU farmers – those with the largest holdings.

Common Fisheries Policy (CFP): The joint aim of the CFP is to protect stocks of fish – and fishing communities. Forty years after its introduction, critics say it has failed on both counts. According to Debating Europe, it is a system that favours the big boys. At the heart of it is what is known as "quota hopping" – the practise by which a fishery in one EU country registers part of its business in another EU country, thus taking part of the latter country's fishing quota. (Britain originally approved the practise, though its fishermen now bitterly resent it.) Within the EU, says Debating Europe, quota hopping "has enabled big commercial fisheries from countries like Spain and Denmark to grab the others' stocks... The system favours big industrial trawlers while penalising small, sustainable inshore fishing." Meanwhile, wasteful rules forcing the dumping of billions of dead fish because they are either too small or the "wrong" species indicate a bureaucracy run amok.

A national fishing policy would allow local fleets to respond more flexibly. The counter-argument is that "fish don't follow frontiers" – therefore, a common policy to manage fisheries and protect stocks from competition between national fleets is clearly crucial. Whatever the case, UK membership of the EU has coincided with the steady decline of our fishing industry. A 2016 Commons Library report notes that numbers of UK fishermen has halved from 22,134 in 1975, to 11,845 in 2014. Total landings, meanwhile, peaked at 1.0m tonnes in 1973 and have now stabilised at around 0.4m tonnes, "the lowest levels of any years outside the two world wars".

Convergence criteria: the tests national economies have to pass to become eligible to join the single currency.

ECB: the European Central Bank based in Frankfurt,

responsible for ensuring financial stability in the Eurozone. Sets interest rates, issues banknotes and conducts foreign exchange operations. The current president is Mario Draghi.

Ecu: Europe's first quasi-currency. Established with the Exchange Rate Mechanism in 1979.

ERM: Exchange Rate Mechanism A foundation stone of economic and monetary union, providing a central exchange rate for European currencies. Blown apart in 1992 on Black Wednesday when the pound, the Italian lira and the Spanish peseta were forced out.

Euro: the EU's currency. Launched virtually in 1999, and then in cash form in 2002 when national currencies were phased out.

Eurozone: the EU countries that have adopted the euro. 19 out of 28 are currently in the zone. Of the remainder, six – Bulgaria, Croatia, Czech Republic, Hungary, Poland and Romania – say they intend joining but haven't yet qualified. Britain and Denmark secured opt-outs in 1992, Sweden voted to reject the euro in 2003.

European Commission: the main executive body of the EU (see Ch 6: How the EU Works).

European Parliament: the only directly elected assembly in the EU (see Ch 6: How the EU Works).

EU Directive: a form of legislation "directed" at member states, which must then pass the relevant domestic legislation to give effect to its terms within a given timeframe, usually two years.

Maastricht Treaty: the 1992 treaty that brought the European Union into being and set the blueprint for economic and monetary union. Many member states had difficulties ratifying it.

Qualified Majority Voting: The most common method of decision-making in the Council of Ministers: unanimity is only required on the most sensitive issues (see below, Veto). Under QMV each member state is given a certain number of votes in the council, weighted by size and population.

Schengen Agreement: eliminates many of the EU's internal borders to allow for passport-free movement. Initially signed by Belgium, France, Germany and Luxembourg in 1985, it now stretches across 26 countries, including non-EU states like Norway and Iceland. Britain and Ireland have remained outside the agreement.

Veto: a country's ability to vote down a decision in the Council of Ministers when the unanimous voting system used for the most nationally sensitive decisions is in use. This embraces decisions on foreign policy, treaty changes, EU funding and tax (except VAT). Eurosceptics worry that the creeping spread of qualified majority voting (see above) removes Britain's ability to apply its veto in important areas: a recent flashpoint was the rules governing banks and financial institutions. In 2014, 95 Conservative MPs urged the Government to give Westminster a national veto to block new EU legislation and repeal existing measures that threaten "national interests". Downing Street rejected the demand saying it would make the single market unworkable.

USING THIS GUIDE IN SCHOOLS
by Richard Addis, founder of

Here is a live issue that involves politics, history, geography, economics, languages, art, literature and citizenship -- in short, a huge range of the national curriculum.

It is also the most significant vote in the UK for the past 40 years.

Anyone under 18 may not vote: but The Day believes that teenagers should work out where they stand and register their views on our online poll so that we can inform our political leaders what British teenagers think.

(They can also put quite legitimate pressure on parents and guardians to represent them. It is today's children, after all, who will have to live longest with the consequences of June 23rd.)

Before the rest of the country votes, we will be delivering a letter to David Cameron with detailed feedback from UK schools and with the results of our poll.

We suggest all students in years 12 and 13 are given a copy of this short guide. As far as we are aware, it is the only topical book available that puts forward both sides of the argument in a lucid, balanced, comprehensive fashion.

What a great subject for a debate held before the whole school in early to mid June. And how impressive it would be if young Britons were given a chance to take an informed view about the most important referendum of their lives so far.

Details of how to order copies are on our website at
www.theday.co.uk

CG CONNELL GUIDES

Concise, intelligent guides to history and literature

HISTORY GUIDES

The French Revolution* by David Andress
Winston Churchill* by Paul Addison
World War One by Max Egremont
The American Civil War by Adam Smith
Stalin by Claire Shaw
Nelson by Roger Knight
The Glorious Revolution by Ben Wilson
Russia and its Rulers by Simon Dickson
The Tudors by Susan Doran
Napoleon by Adam Zamoyski
From Addison to Austen by Oliver Cox
The US Civil Rights Movement by Stephen Tuck
The Rise and Fall of the Third Reich by Caroline Sharples
The Cold War by Jeffrey Michaels

* Available now. The rest of the selection above, and other titles, will be available shortly. See www.connellguides.com for details.

"The Connell Guides are brief, attractive, erudite, and to the point. Bravo!"
Sir Tom Stoppard, Playwright

"Connell Guides should be required reading in every school in the country."
Julian Fellowes, creator of Downton Abbey

CONNELL GUIDES TO LITERATURE

Novels and poetry

Emma

Far From the Madding Crowd

Frankenstein

Great Expectations

Hard Times

Heart of Darkness

Jane Eyre

Lord of the Flies

Mansfield Park

Middlemarch

Mrs Dalloway

Paradise Lost

Persuasion

Pride and Prejudice

Tess of the D'Urbervilles

The Canterbury Tales

The Great Gatsby

The Poetry of Robert Browning

The Waste Land

To Kill A Mockingbird

Wuthering Heights

Shakespeare

A Midsummer Night's Dream

Antony and Cleopatra

Hamlet

Julius Caesar

King Lear

Macbeth

Othello

Romeo and Juliet

The Second Tetralogy

The Tempest

Twelfth Night

Modern texts

A Doll's House	Never Let Me Go
A Room with a View	Of Mice and Men
A Streetcar Named Desire	Rebecca
An Inspector Calls	Spies
Animal Farm	The Bloody Chamber
Atonement	The Catcher in the Rye
Beloved	The History Boys
Birdsong	The Road
Hullabaloo	Vernon God Little
	Waiting for Godot

"As with The Week, Connell has the gift of making the daunting and overwhelming accessible and digestible. Yipee!"
Helena Bonham Carter

"Clear, elegant and authoritative guides – worthy of the great masterpieces they analyse."
Robert Harris

"What Connell Guides do is bring immediacy and clarity: brevity with depth. They unlock the complex and offer students an entry route."
Colin Hall, Head of Holland Park School

"The perfect introduction to The Tempest."
Sir Peter Hall, Founder of the Royal Shakespeare Company

"Completely brilliant. I wish I were young again with these by my side. It's like being in a room with marvellous tutors. You can't really afford to be without them, and they are a joy to read."
Joanna Lumley

To buy any of these guides, or for more information, go to
www.connellguides.com
or contact us on (020)79932644 / info@connellguides.com

First published in 2016 by
Connell Guides
Artist House
35 Little Russell Street
London WC1A 2HH

10 9 8 7 6 5 4 3 2 1

Picture credit:
p.11 © LAPI/REX/Shutterstock
p.29 © Central Press/Stringer/Hulton Archive/Getty Images
p.69 © Krisztian Bocsi/Bloomberg/Getty Images

A CIP catalogue record for this book is available from the British Library.
ISBN 978-1-911187-54-7

Design © Nathan Burton
Assistant Editors:
Paul Woodward and Brian Scrivener

Printed by Bell and Bain Ltd, Glasgow

www.connellguides.com